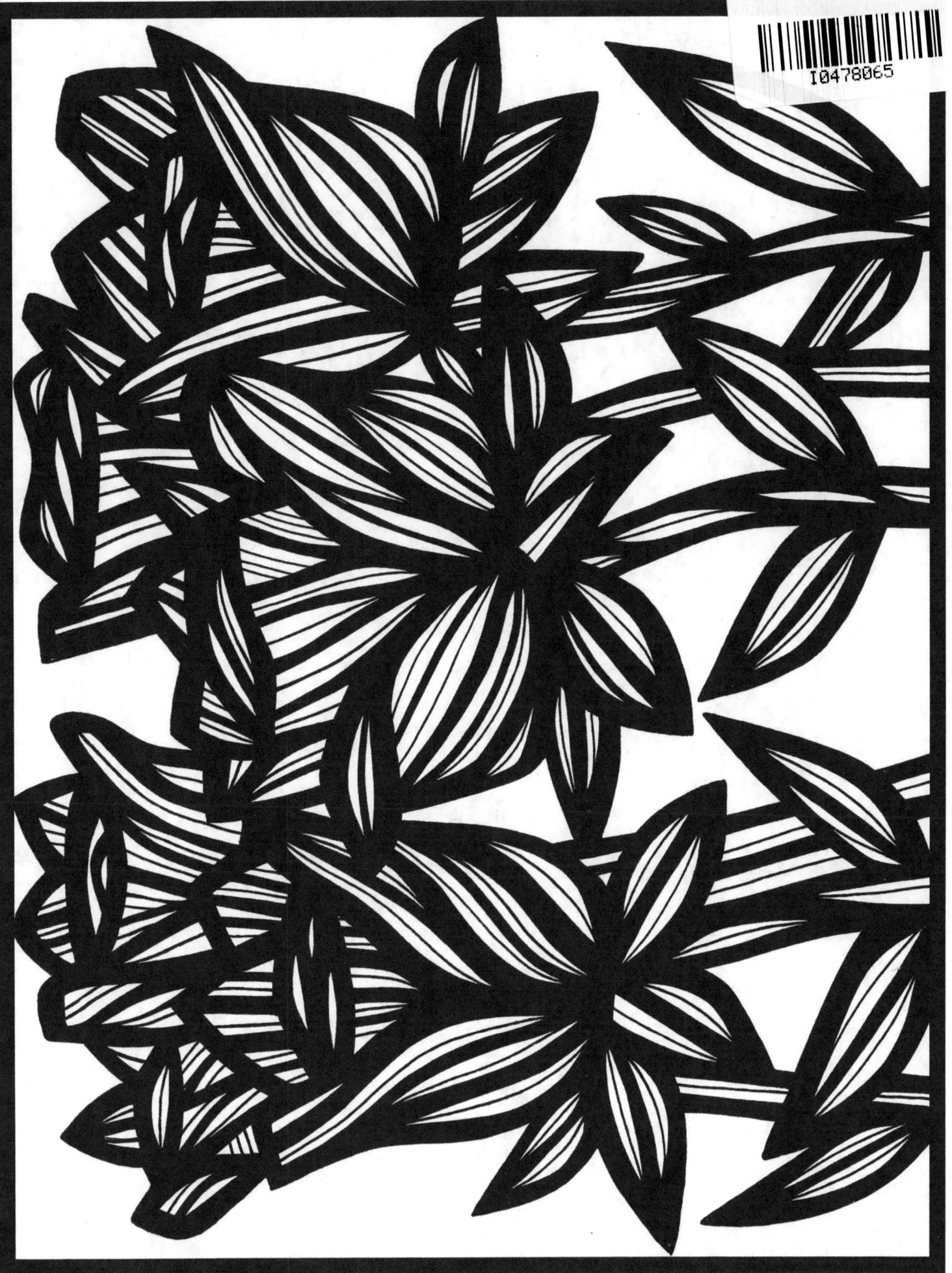

I0478065

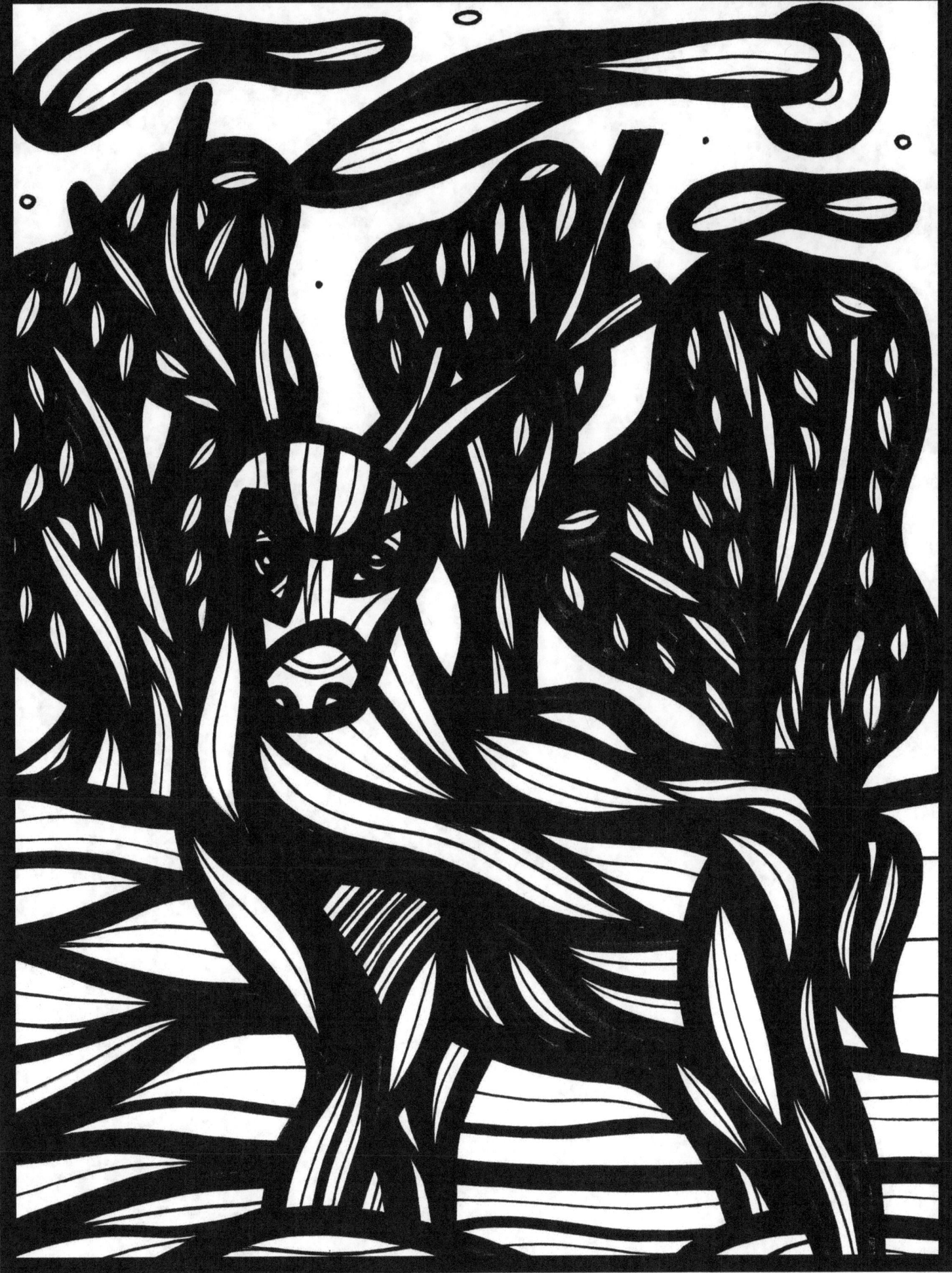

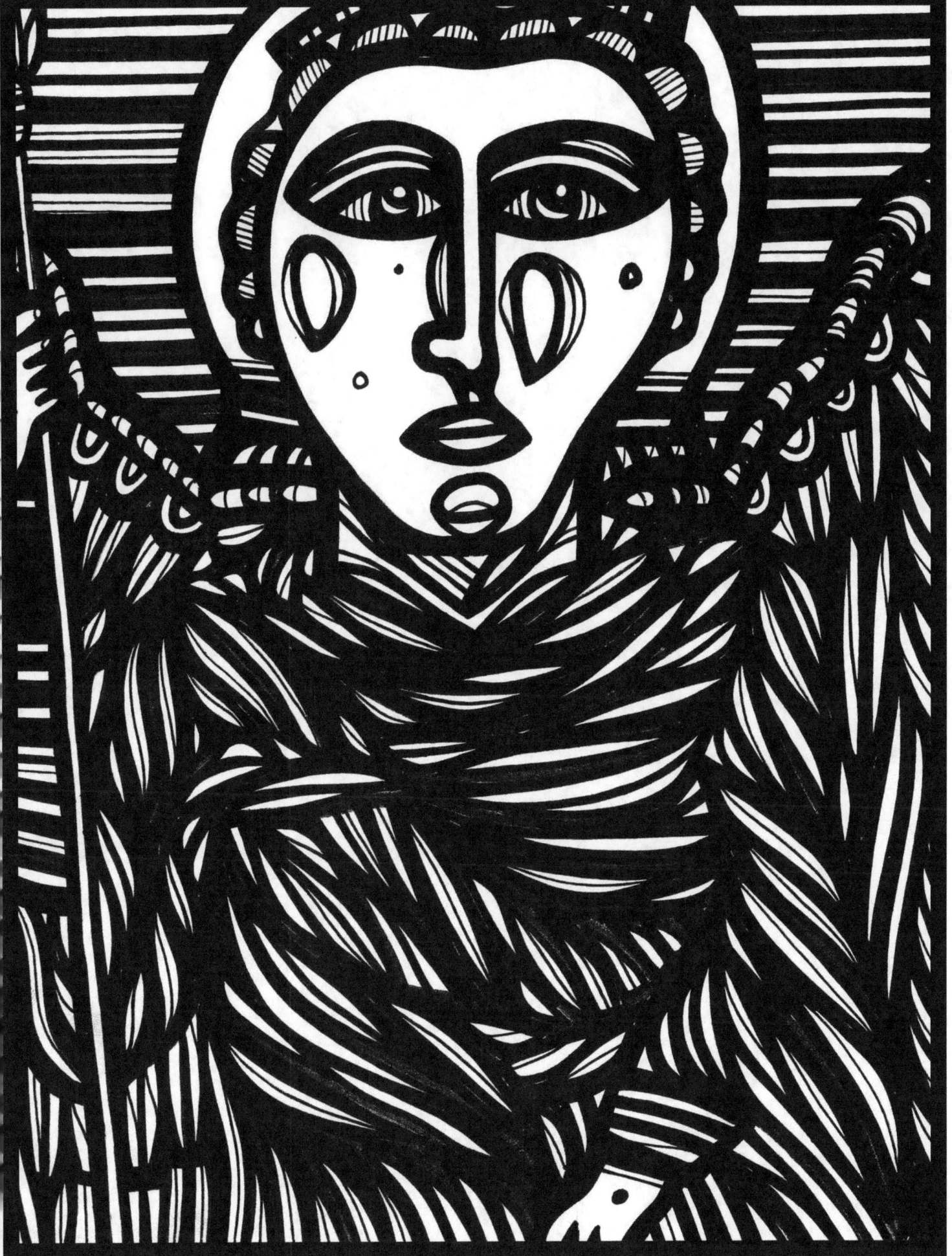

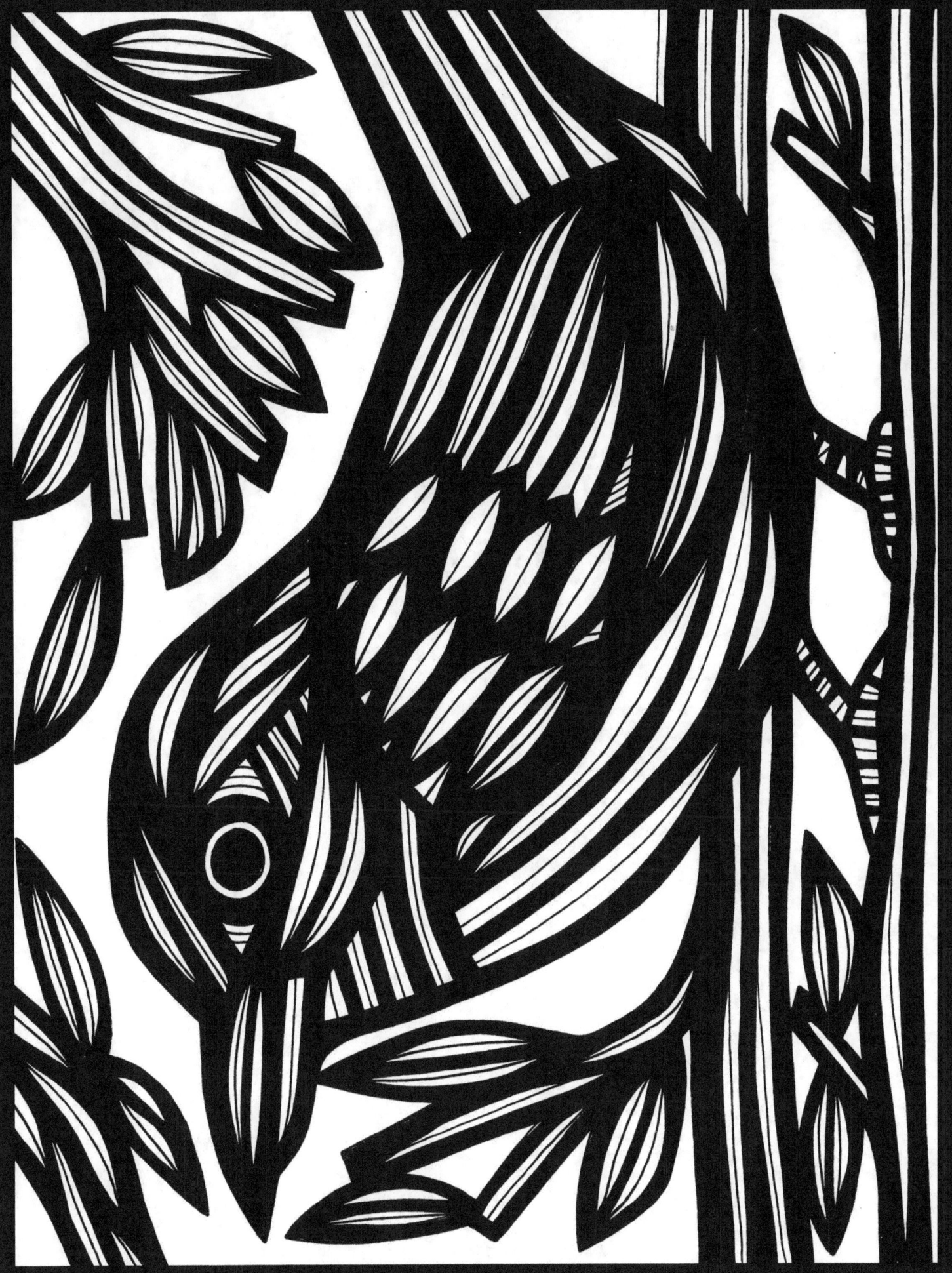

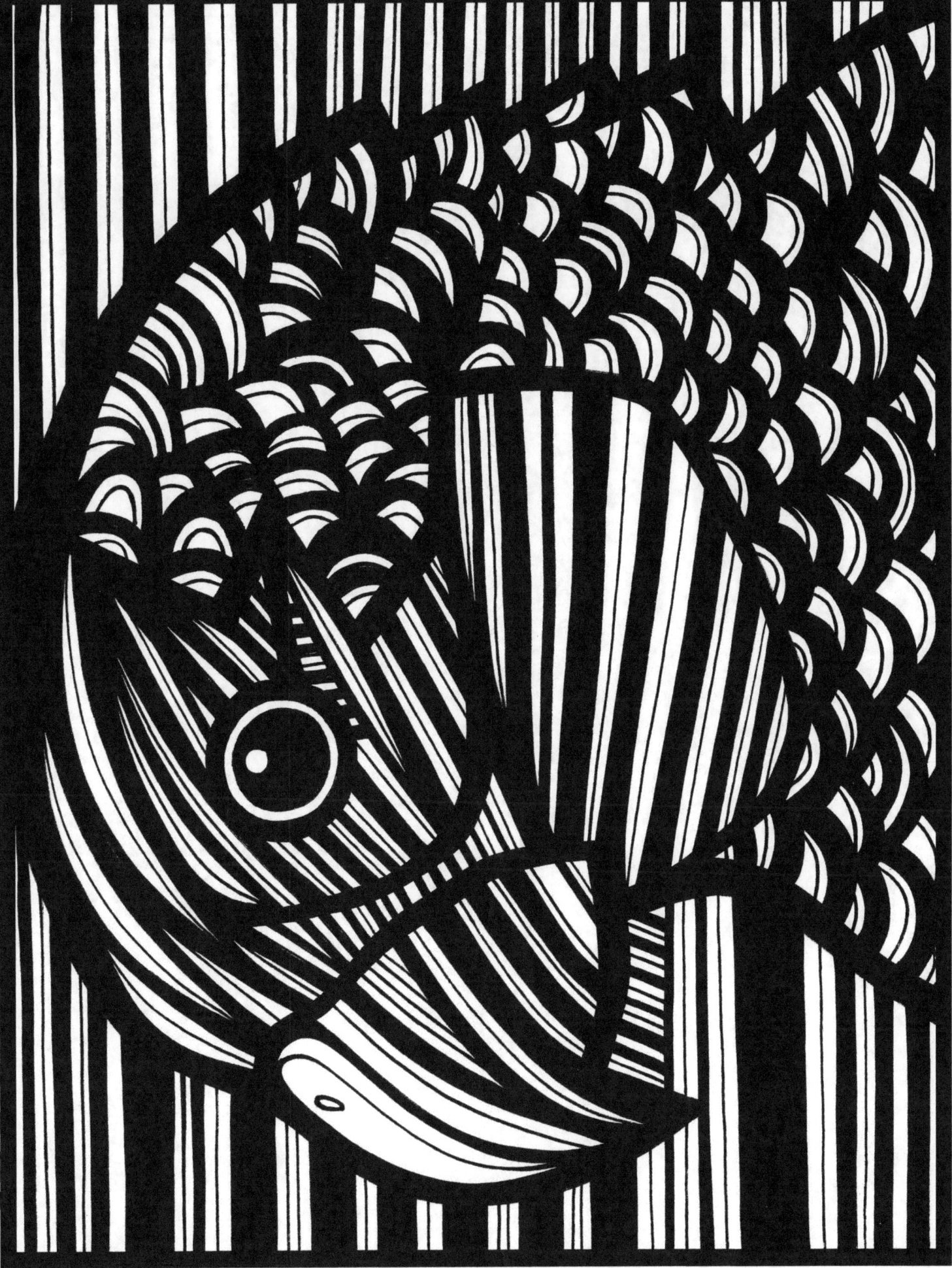

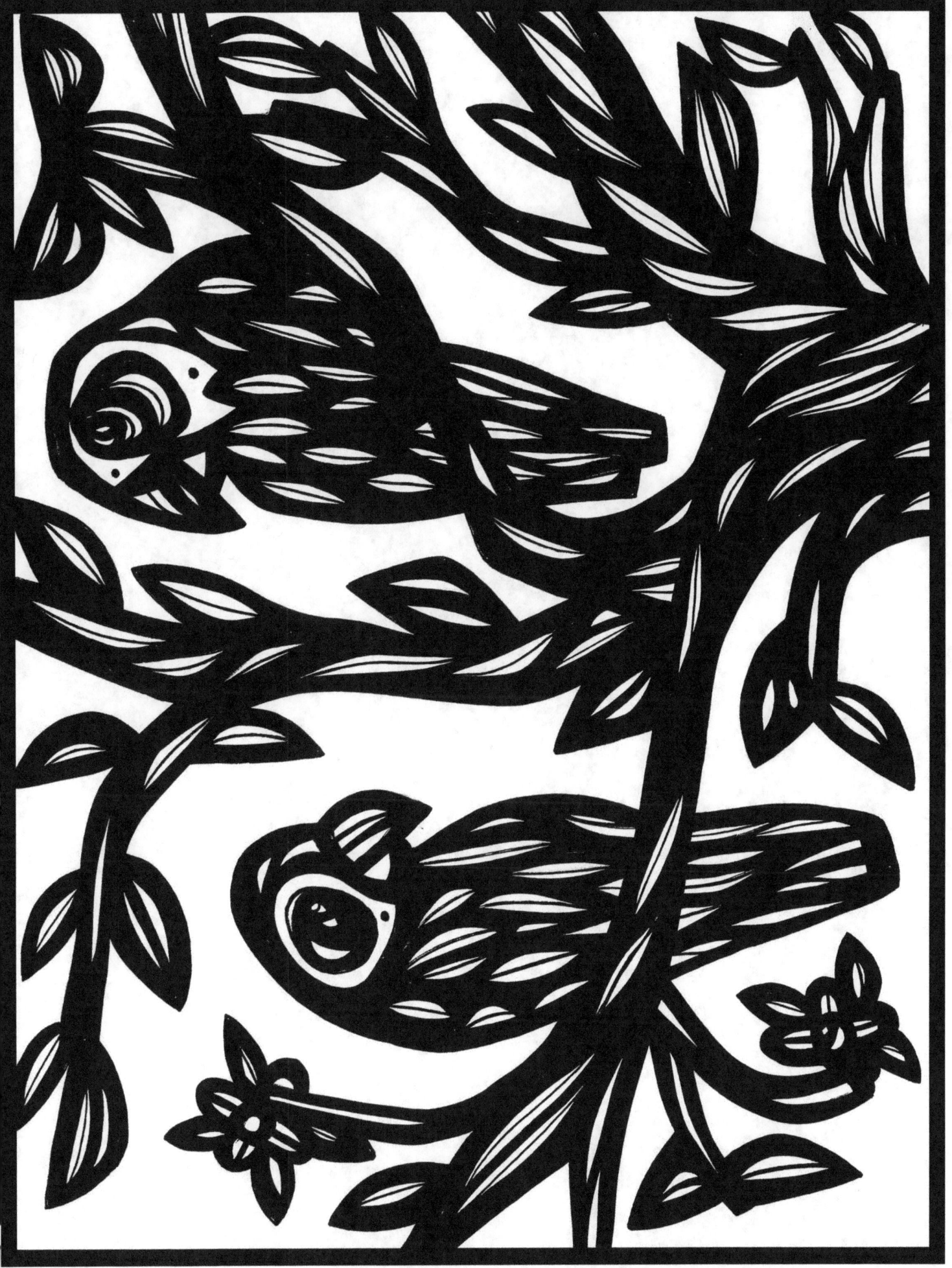

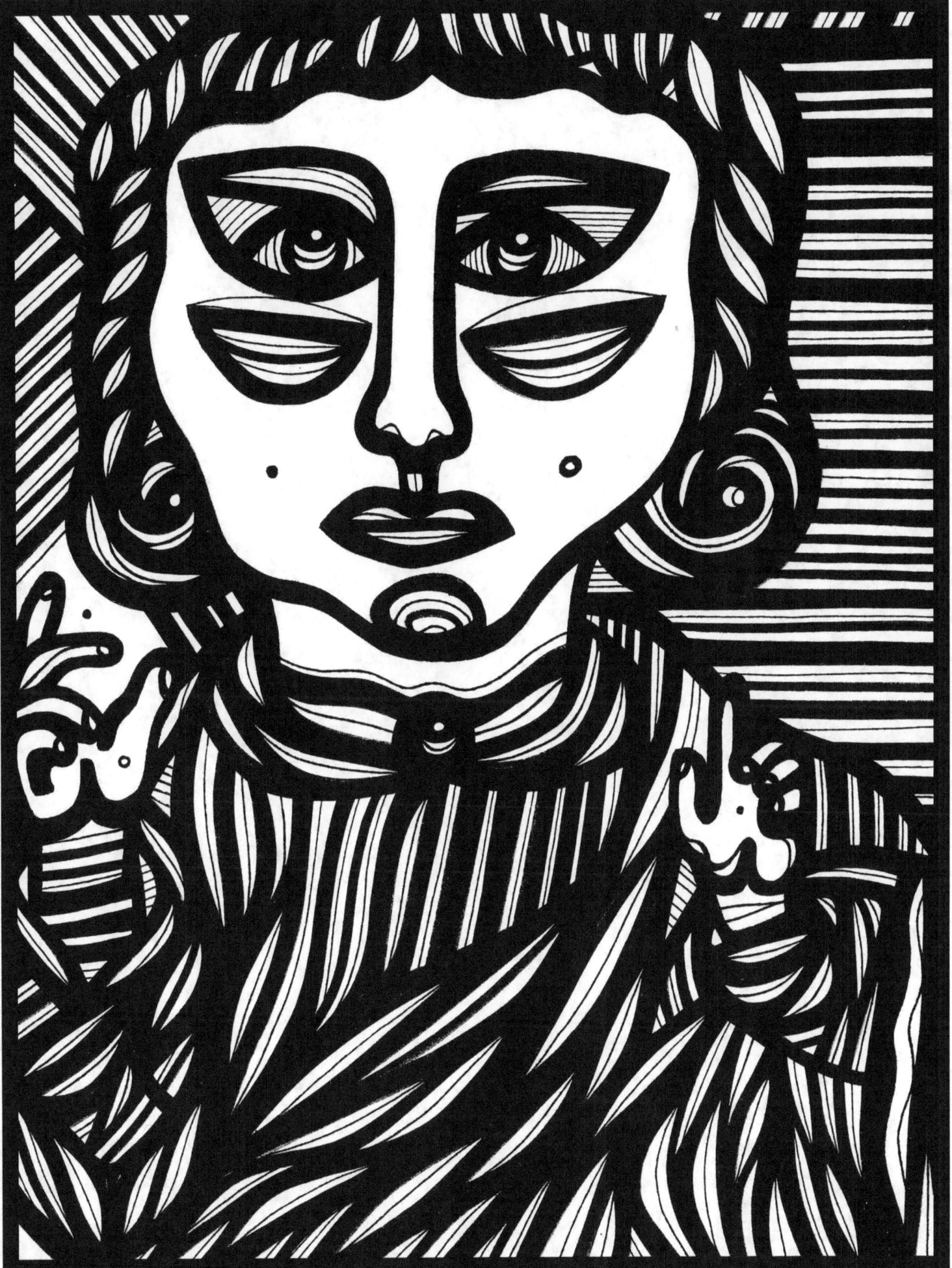

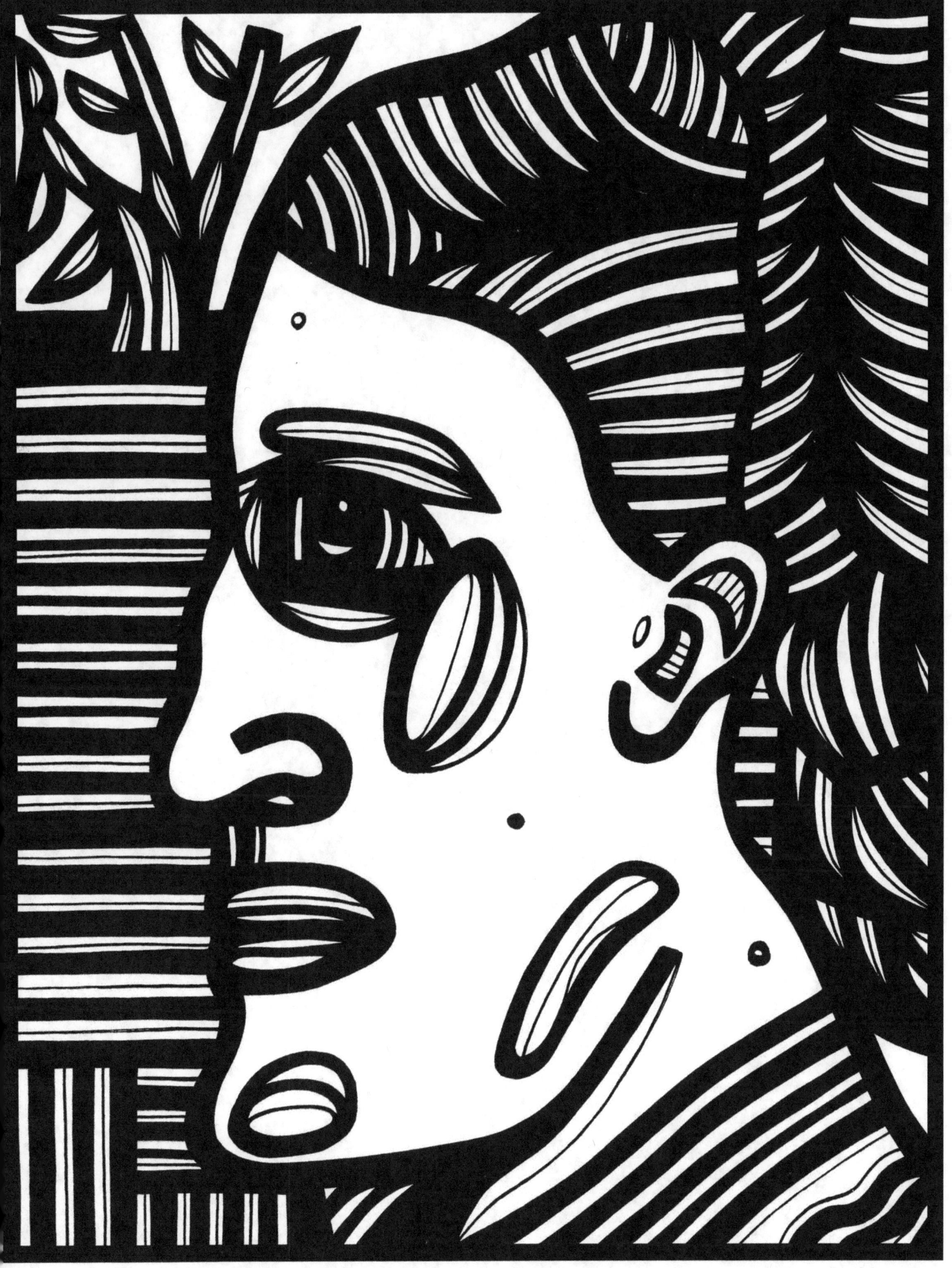

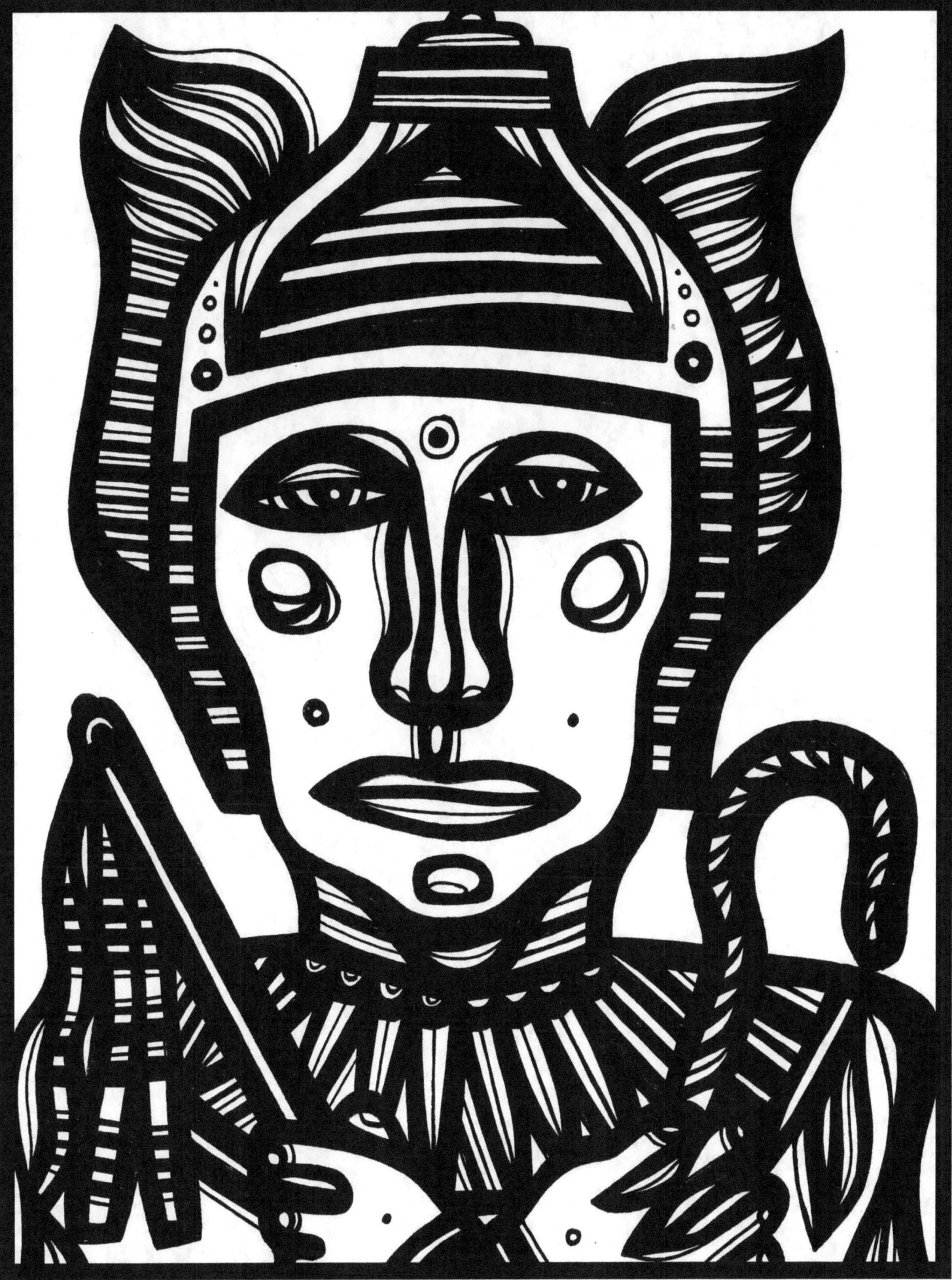

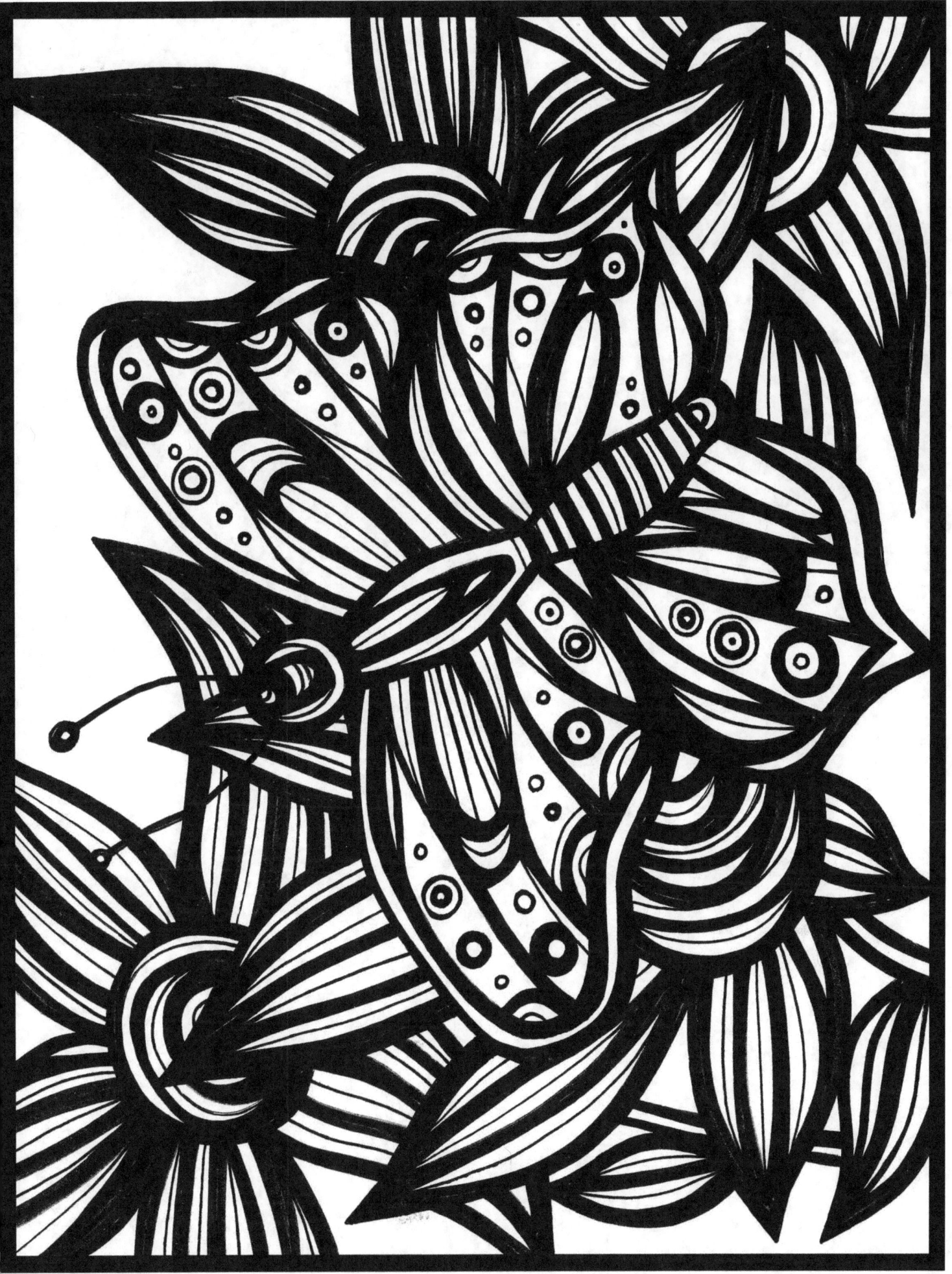

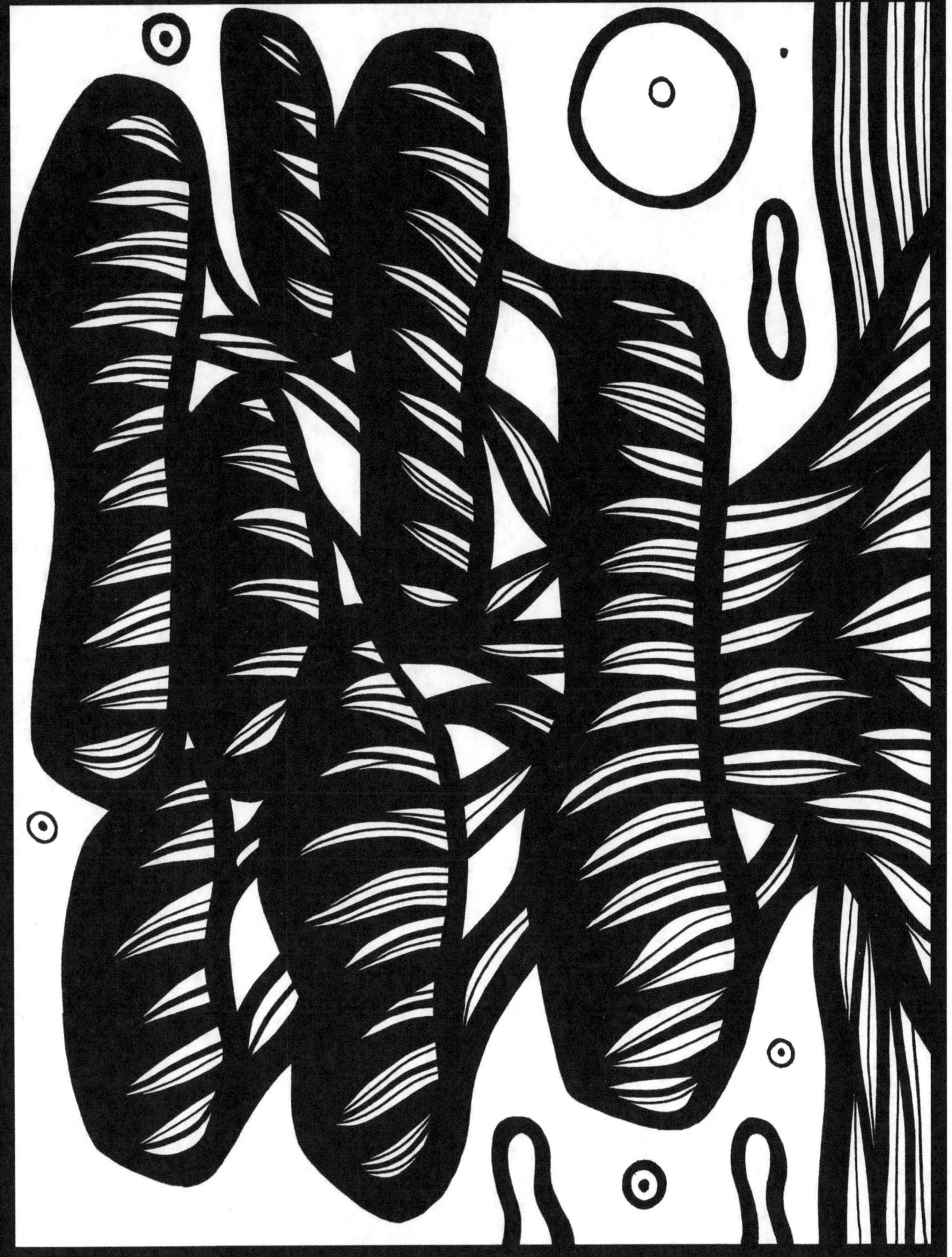

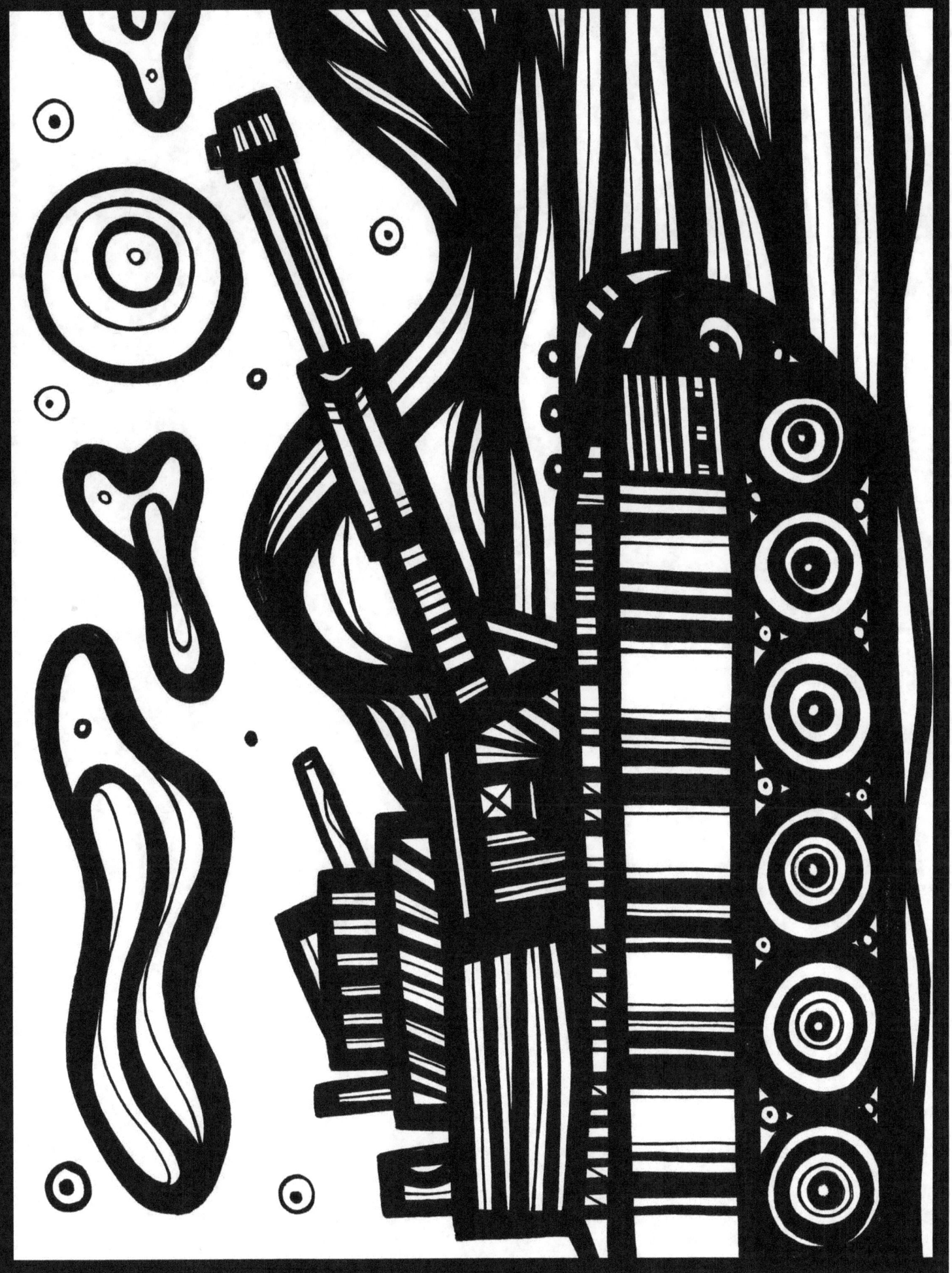

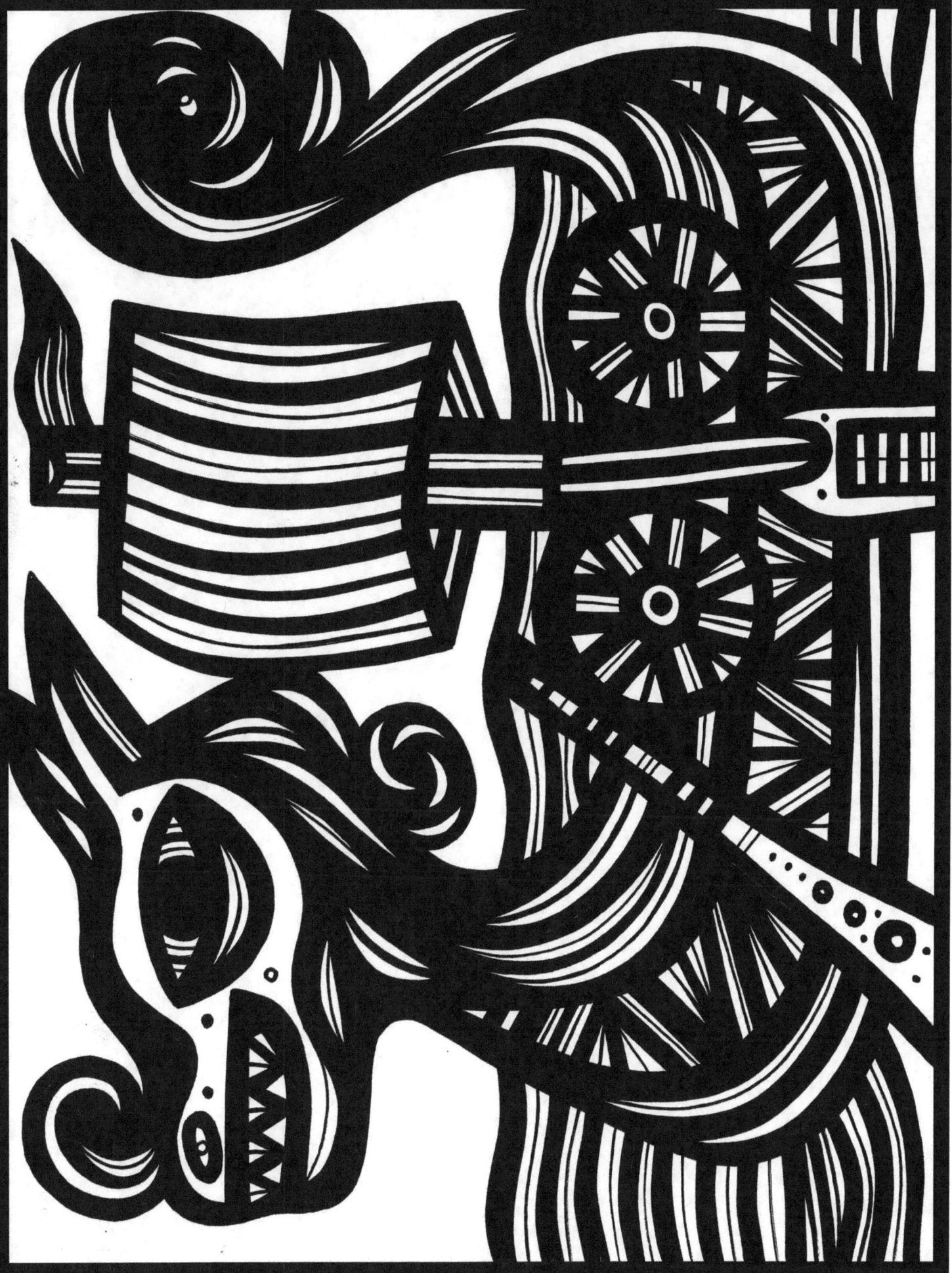

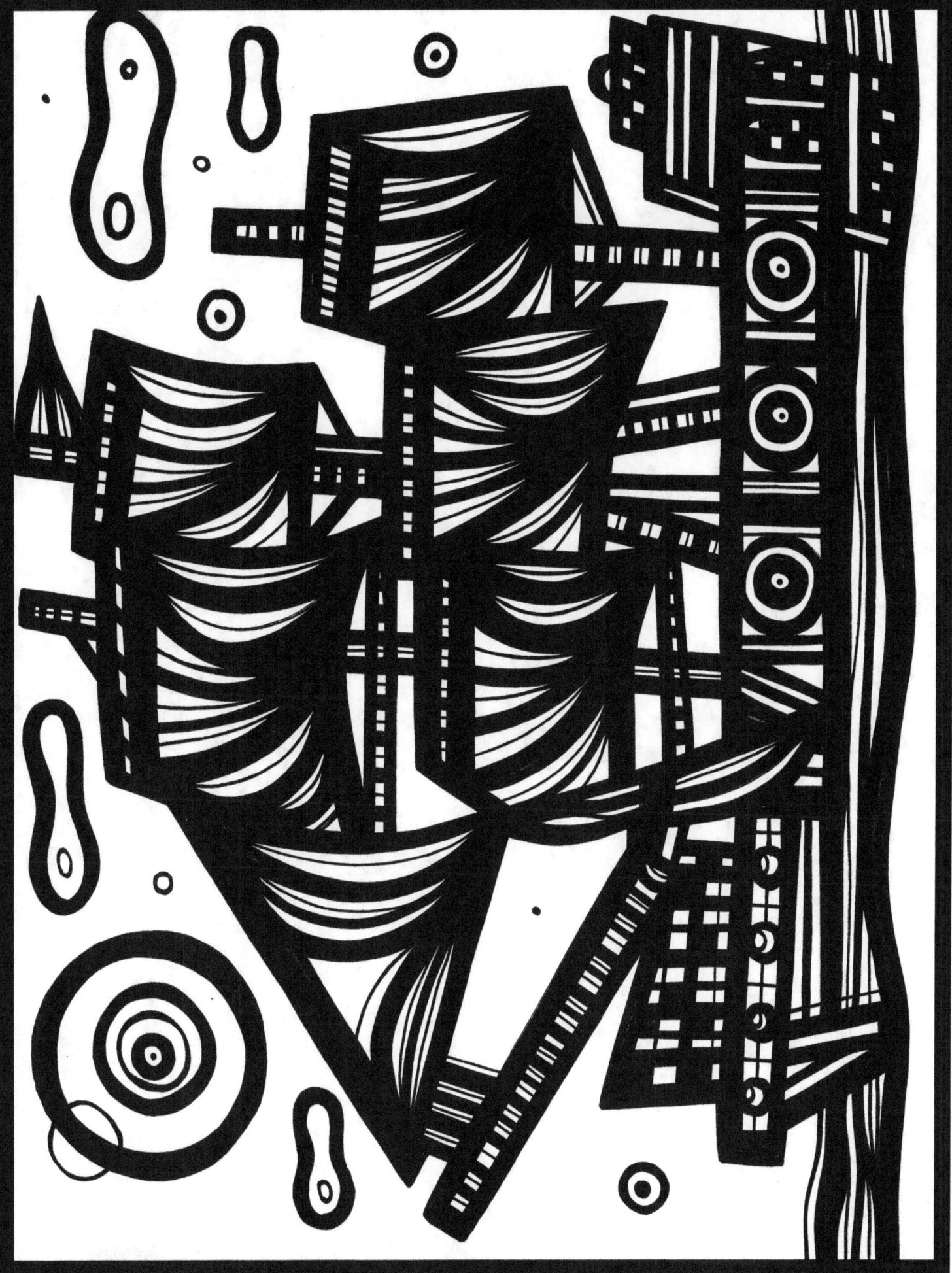

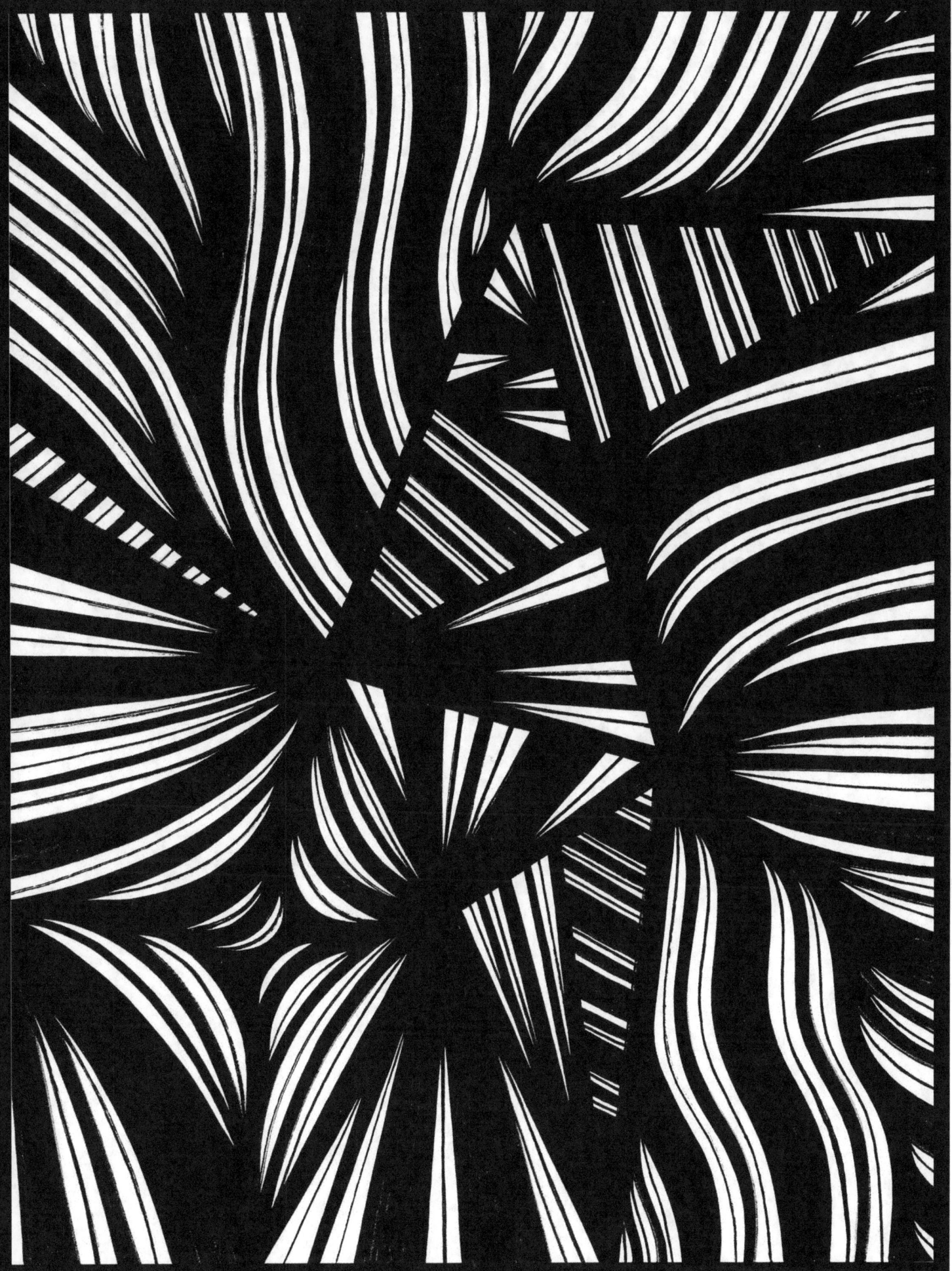

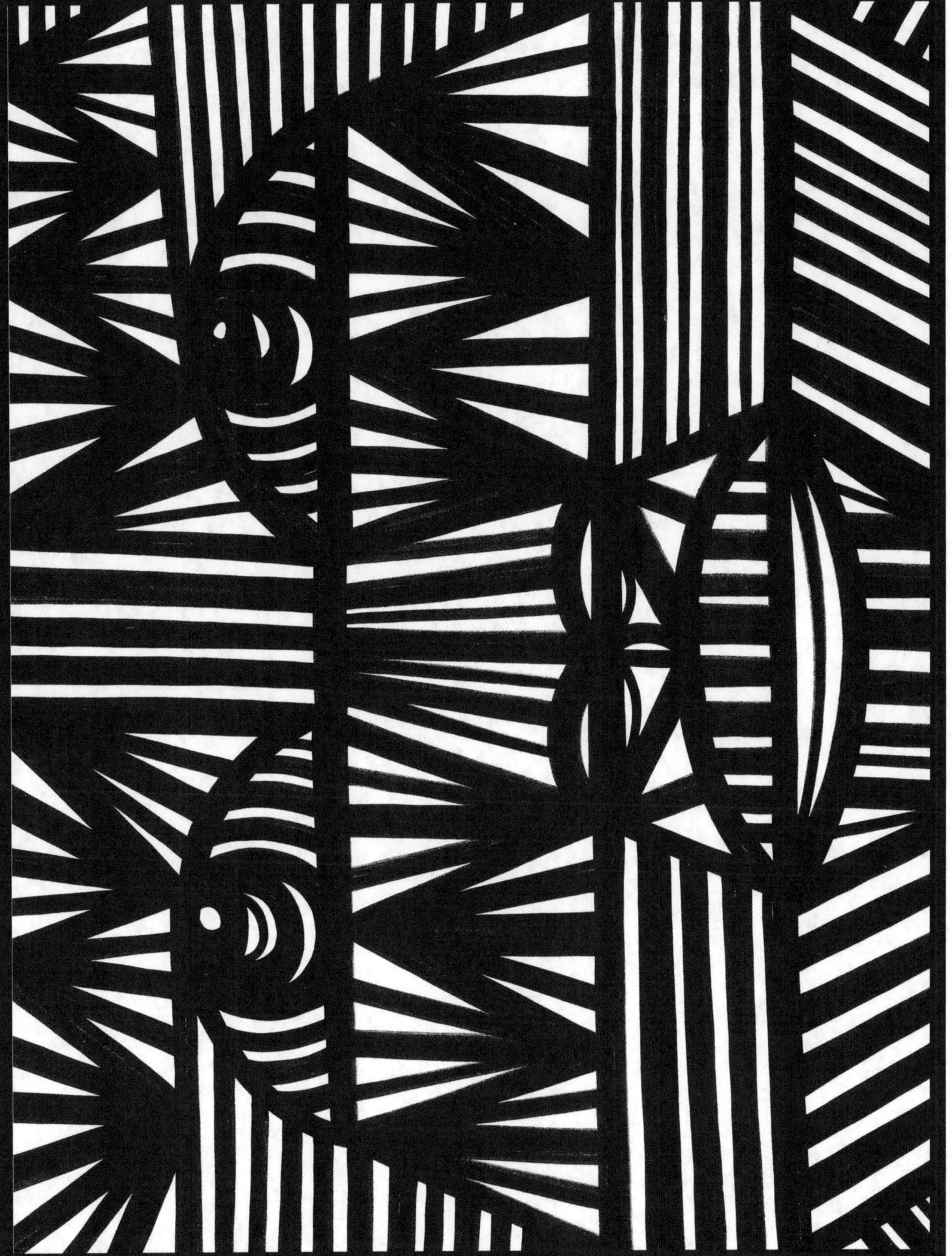

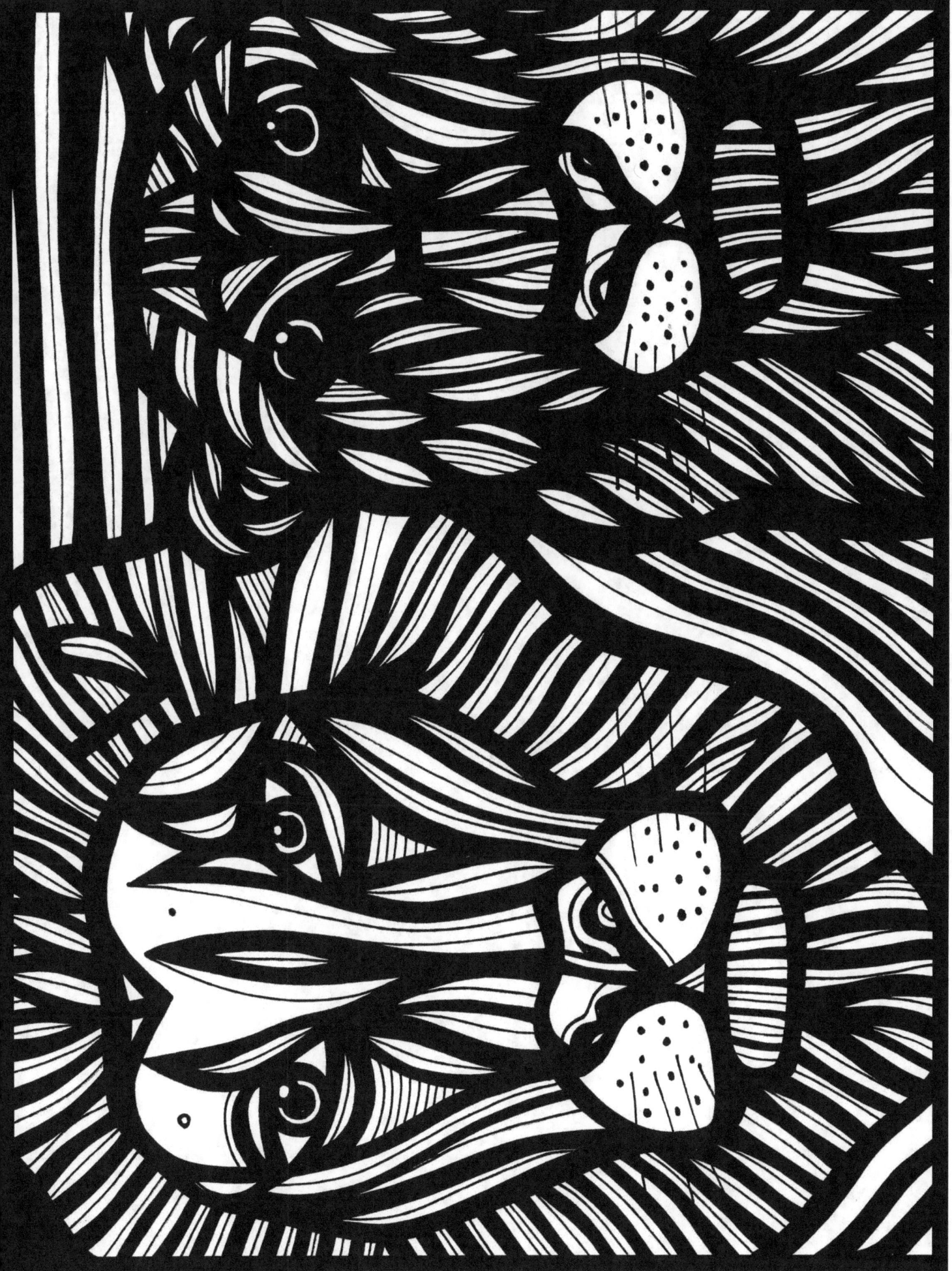

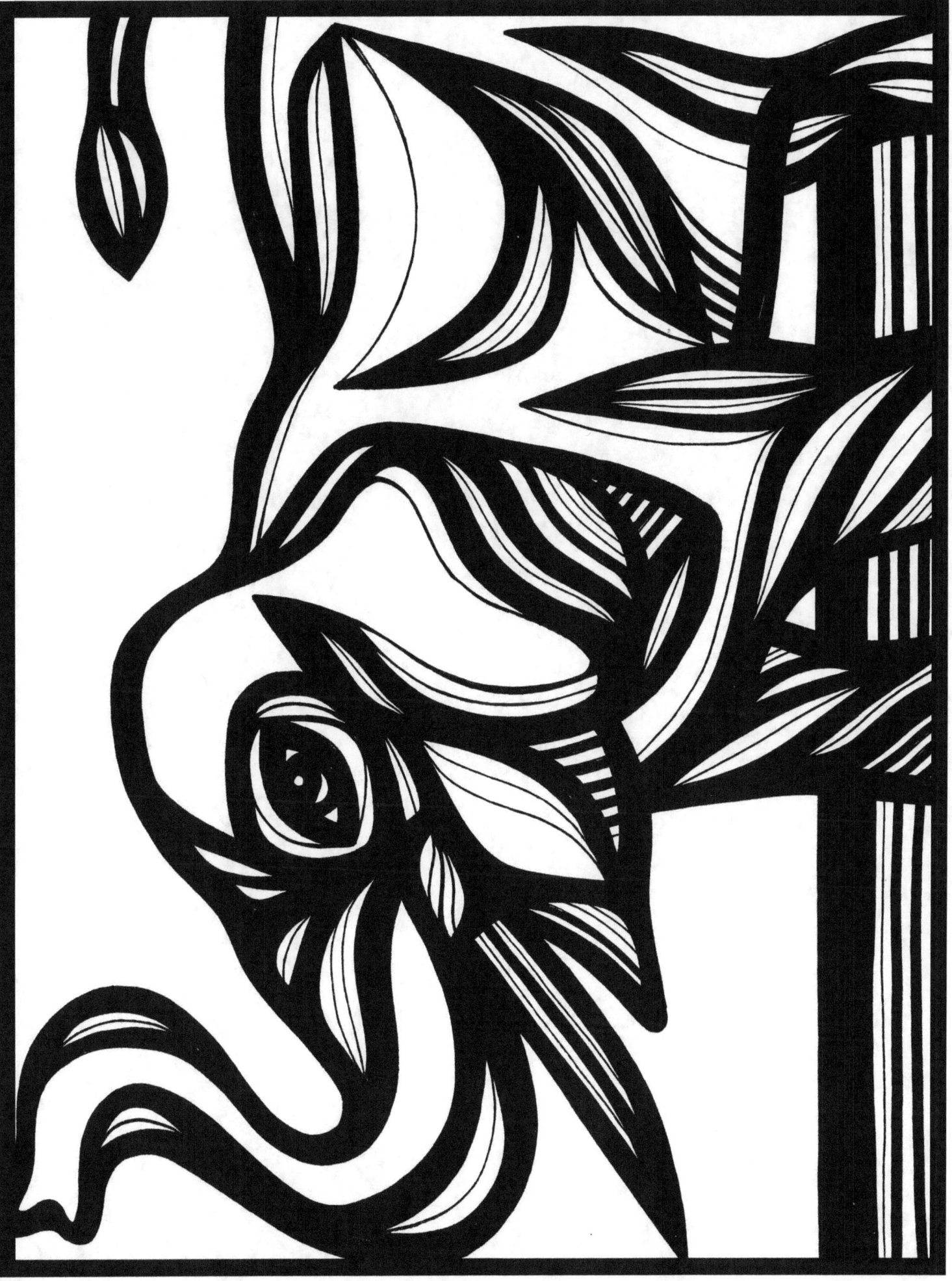

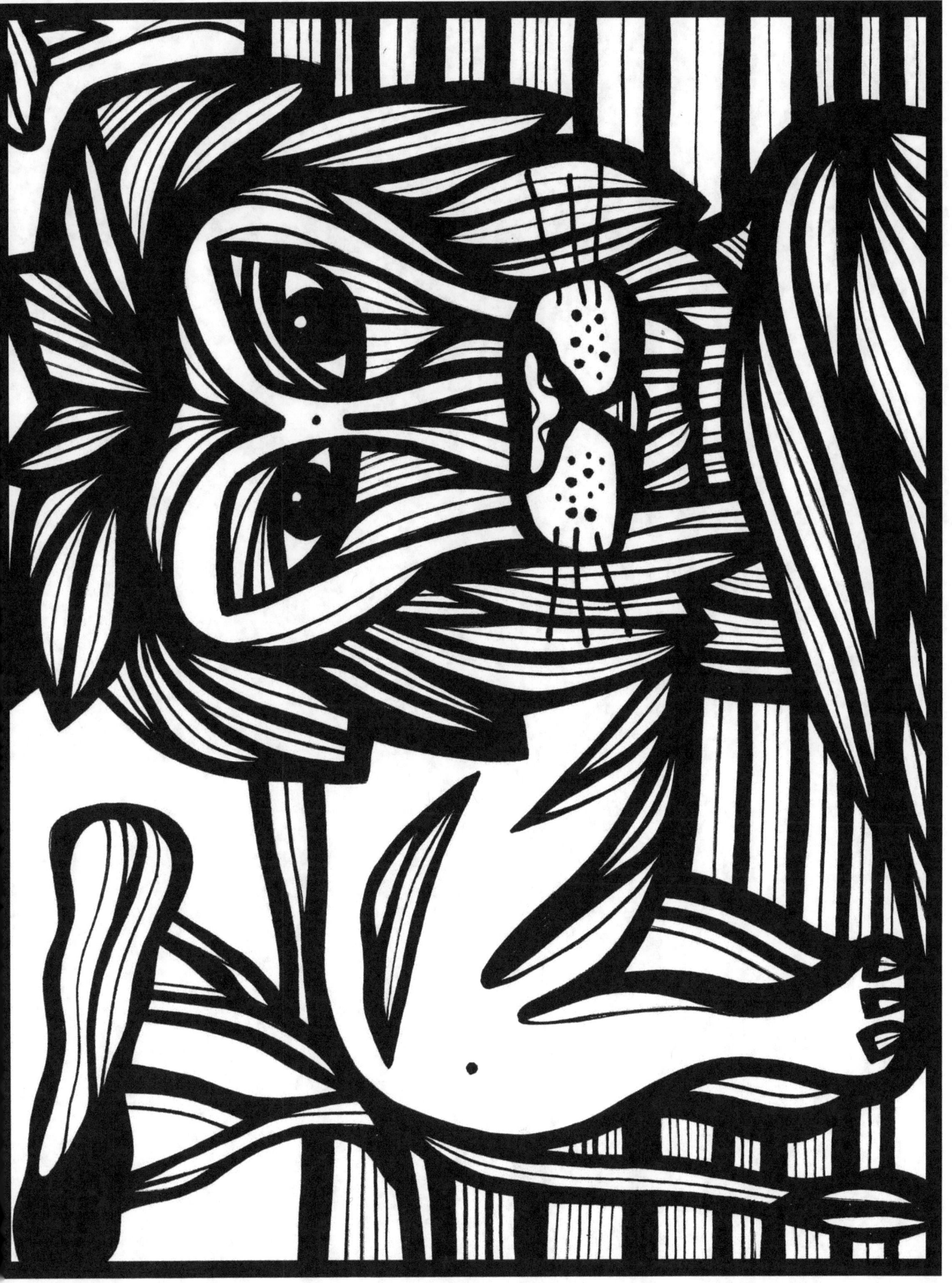

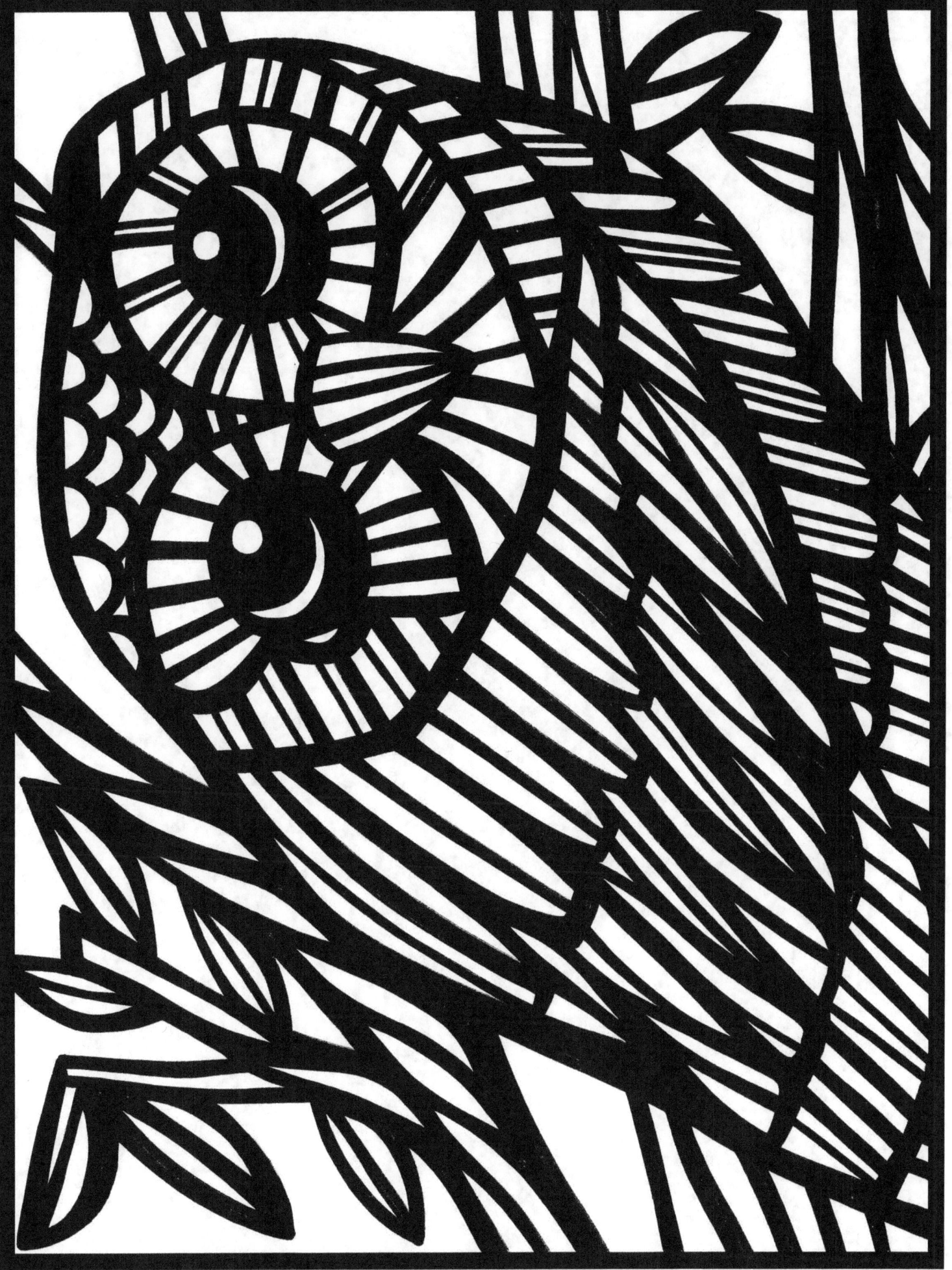

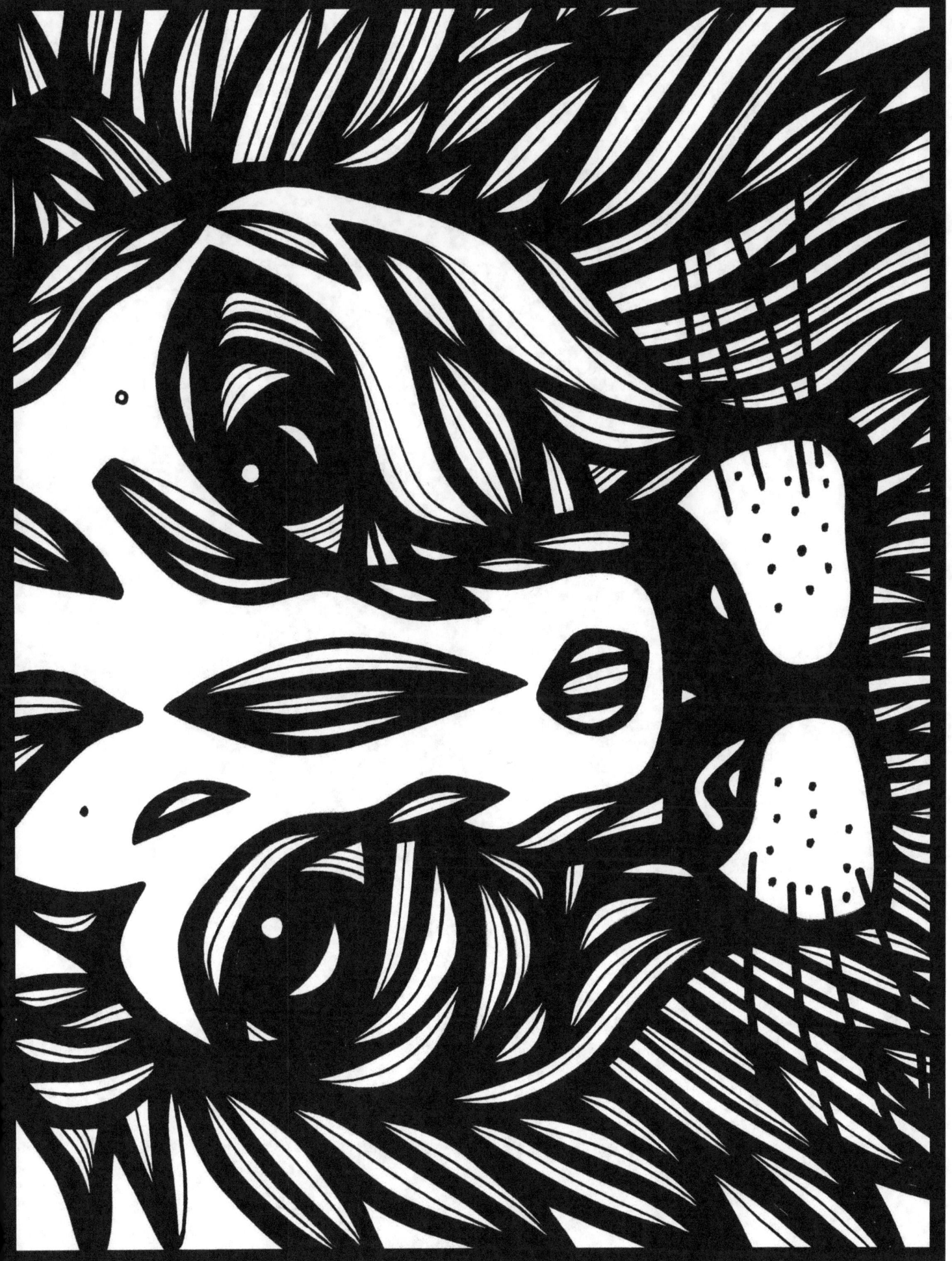

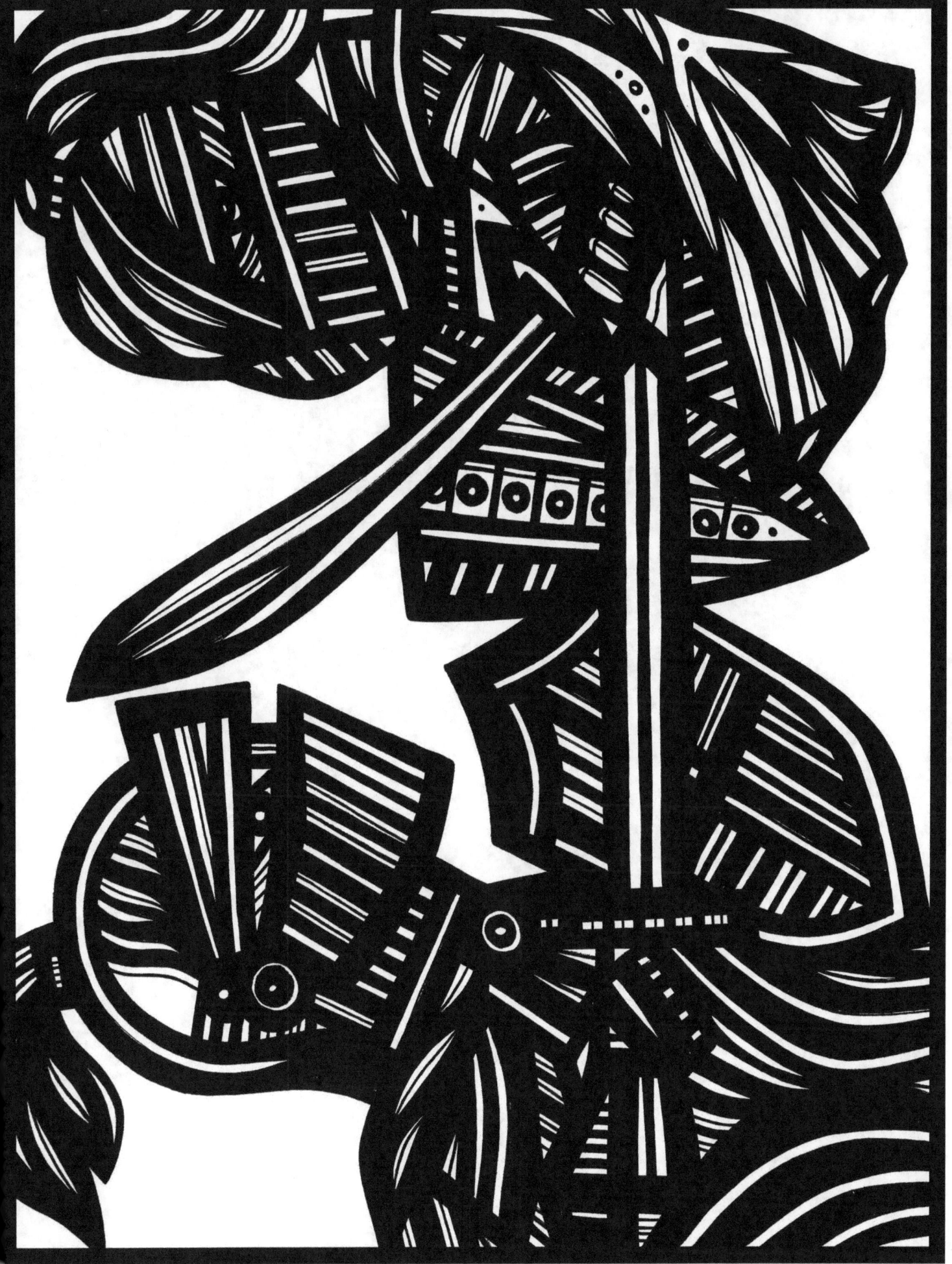

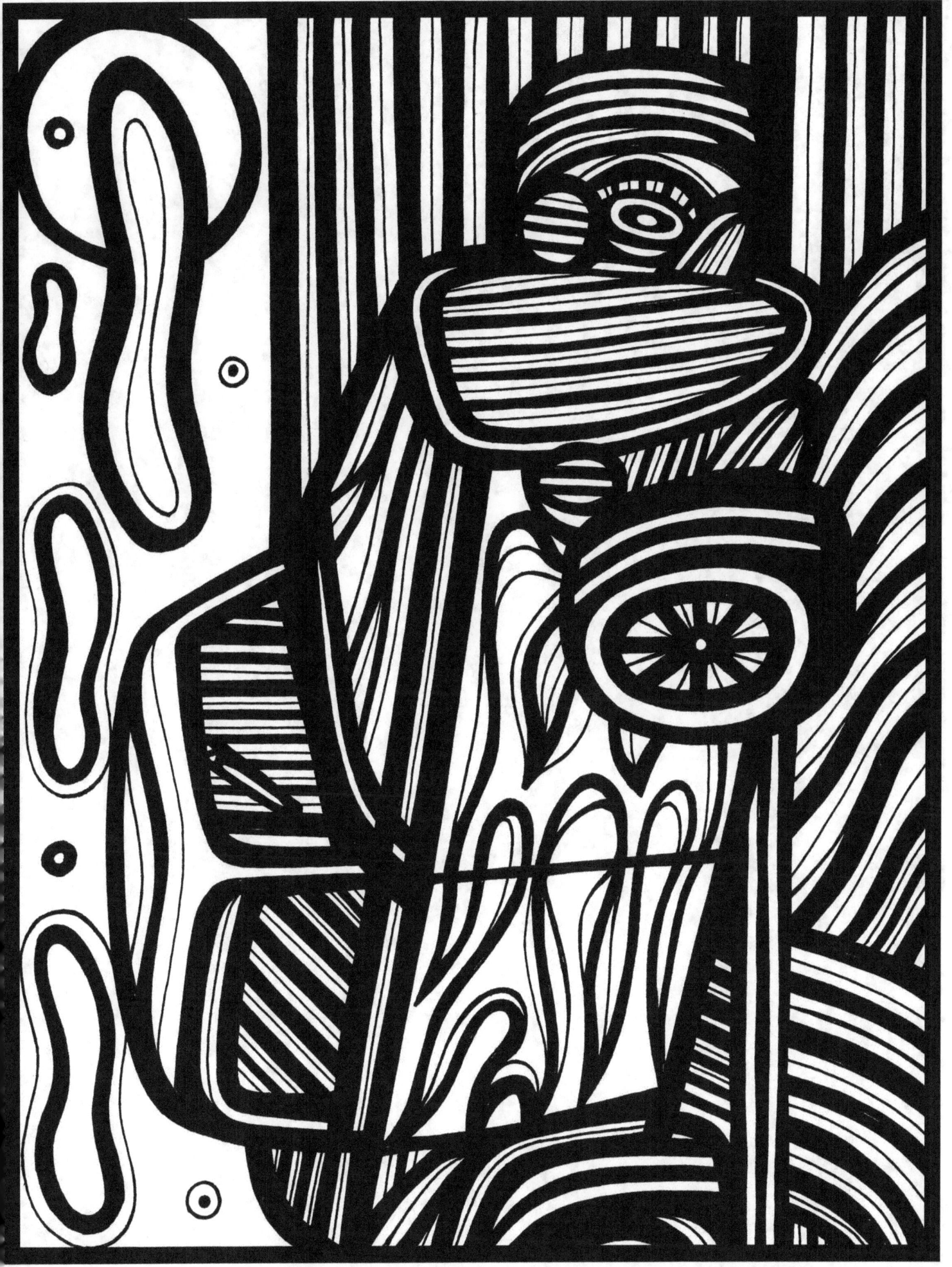

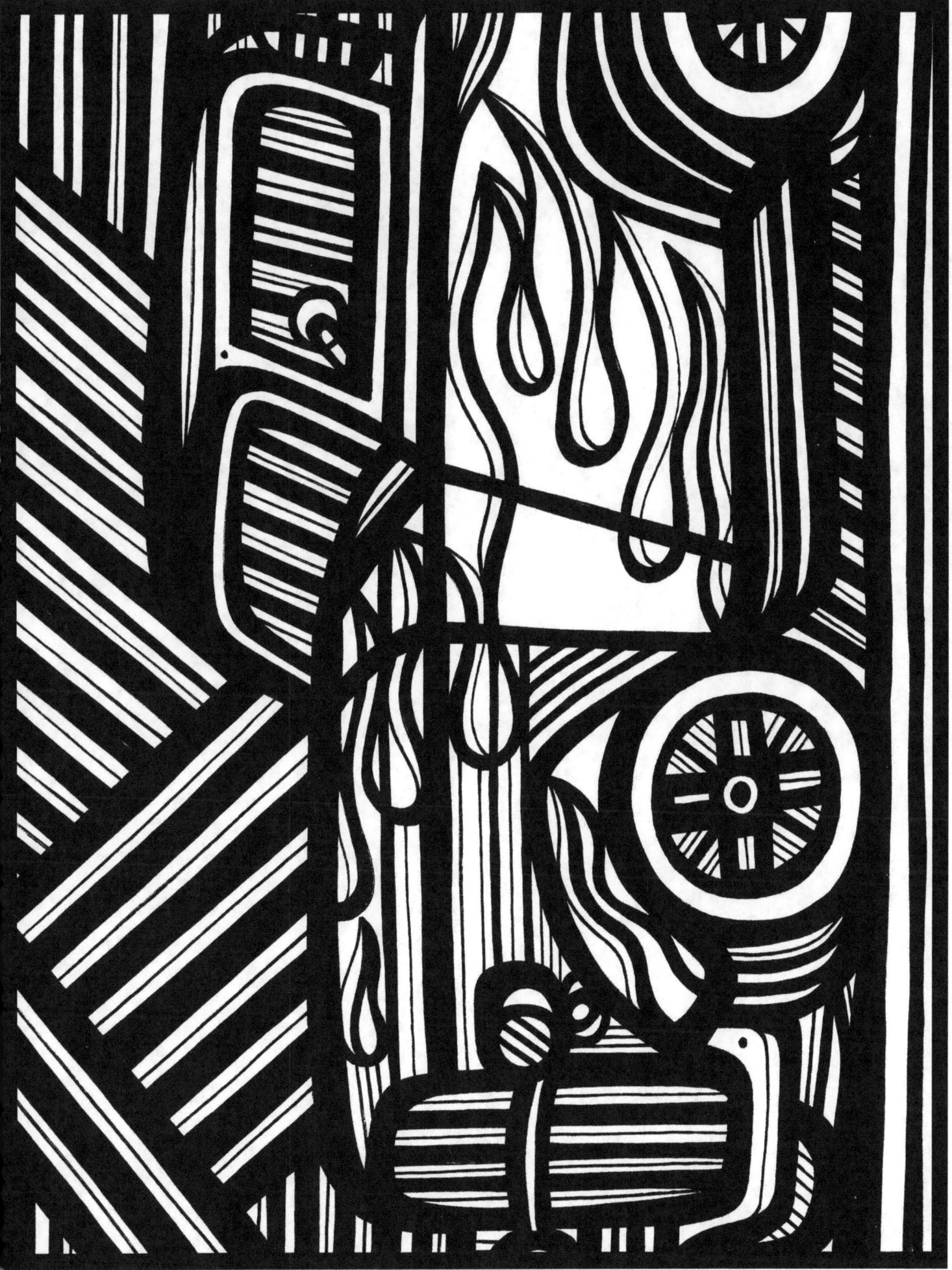

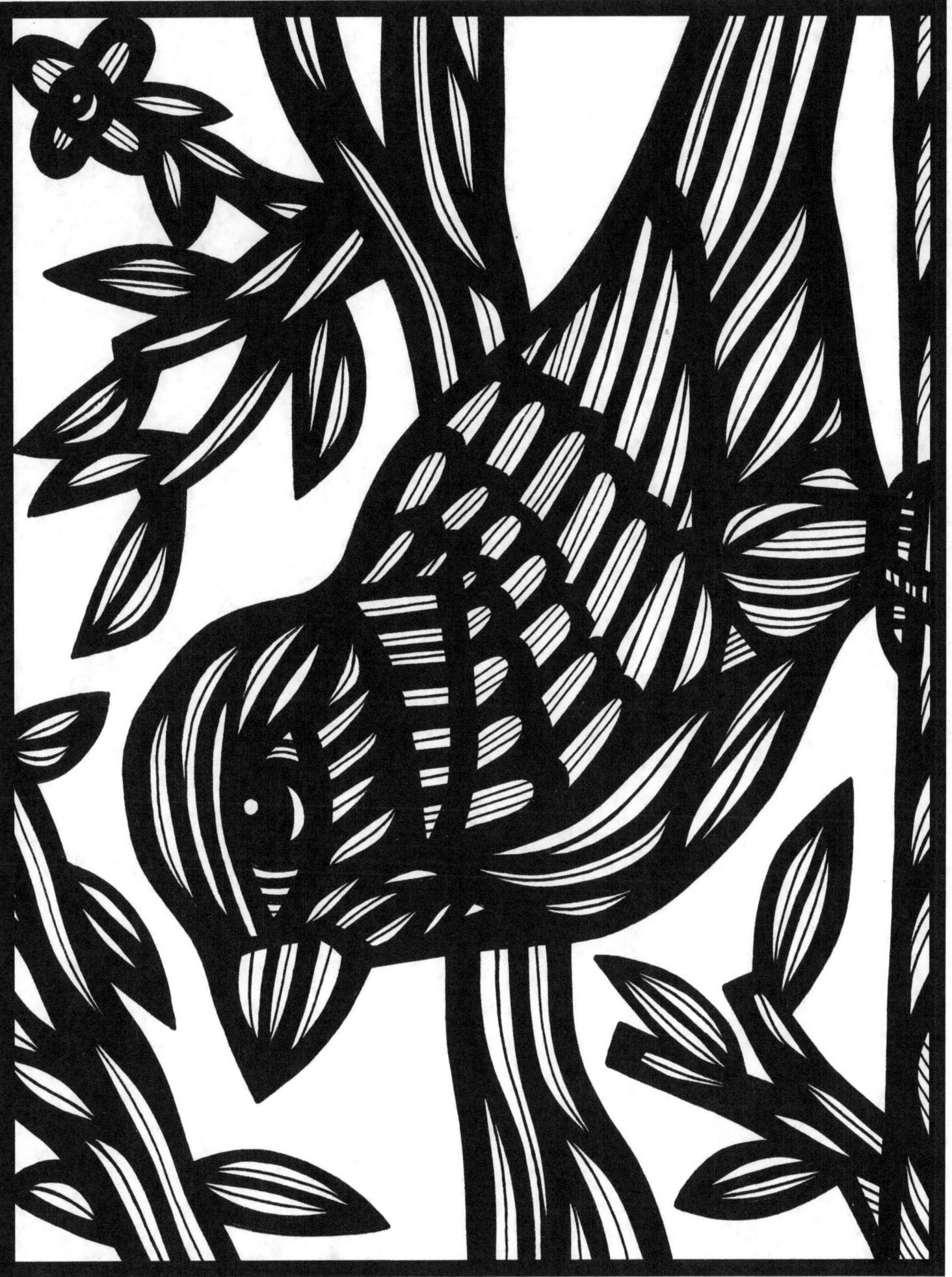

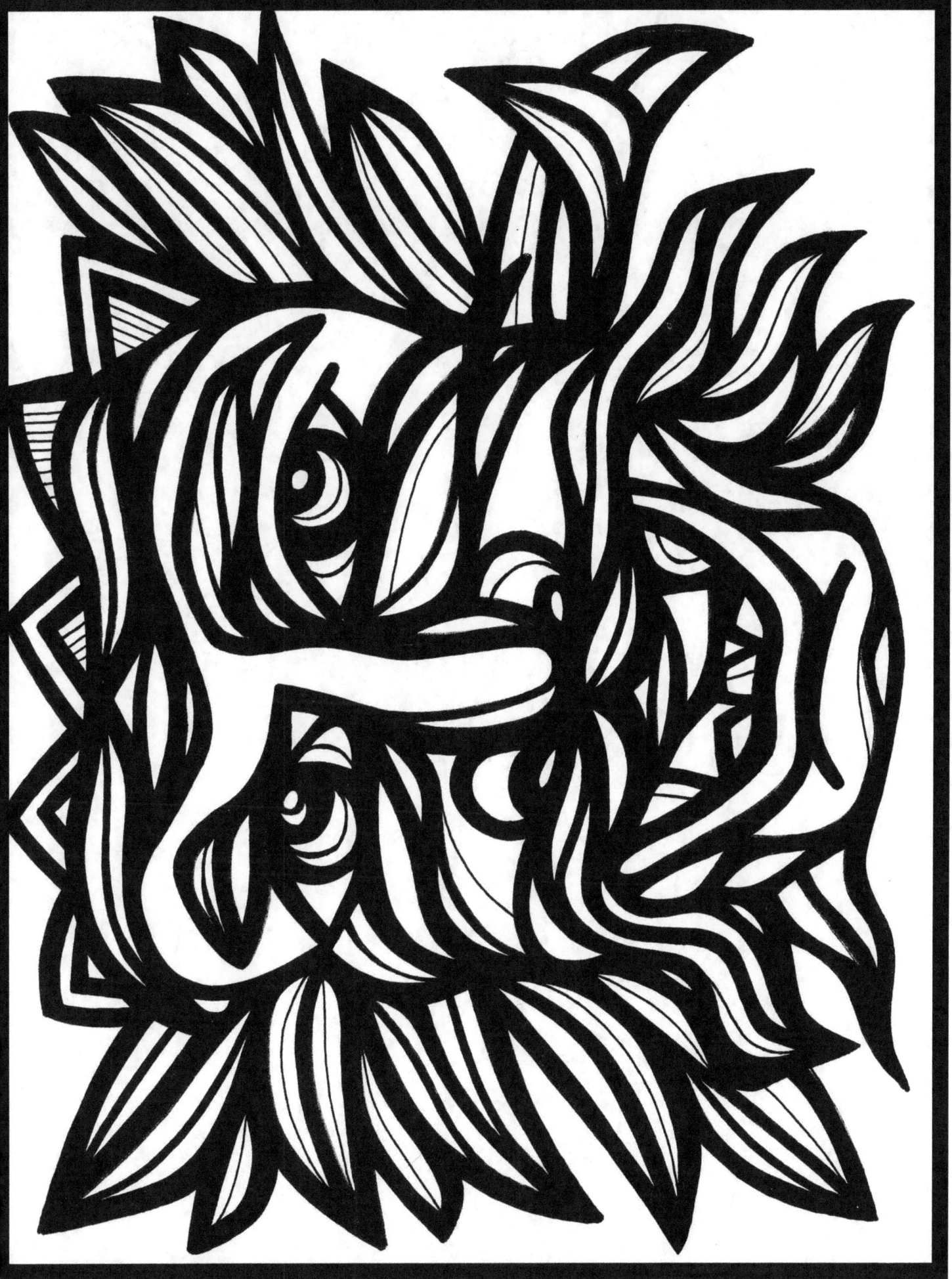

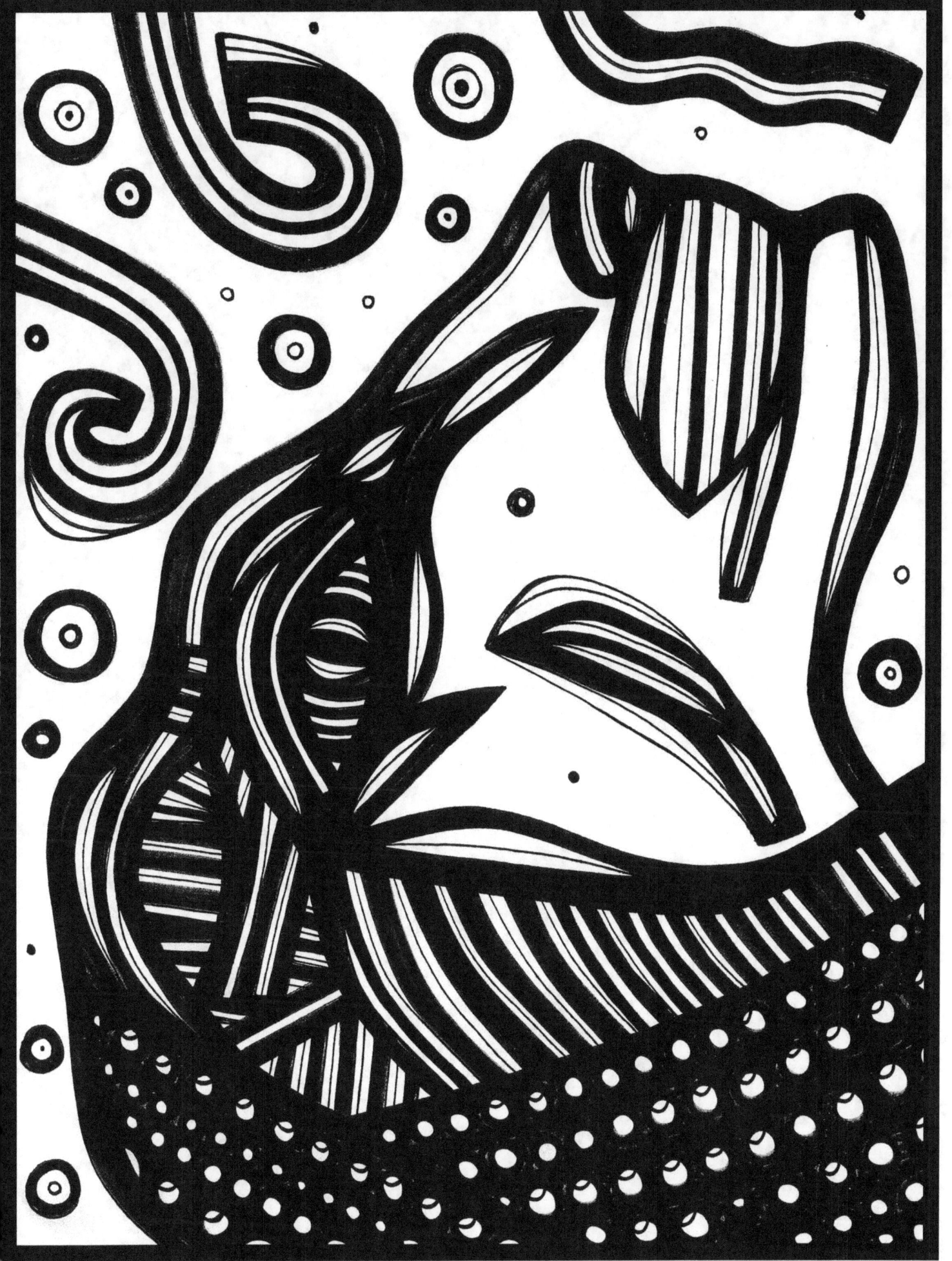

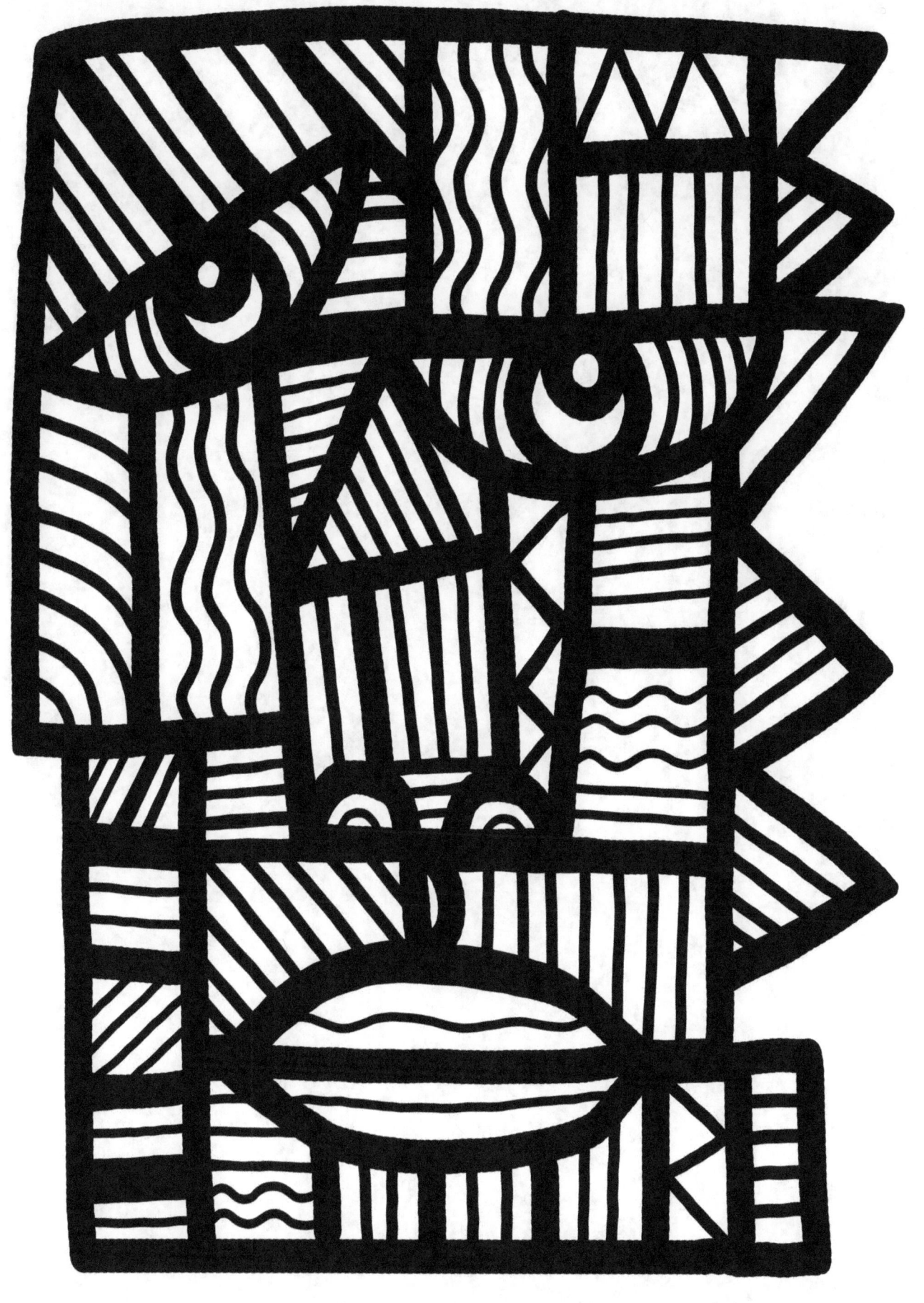

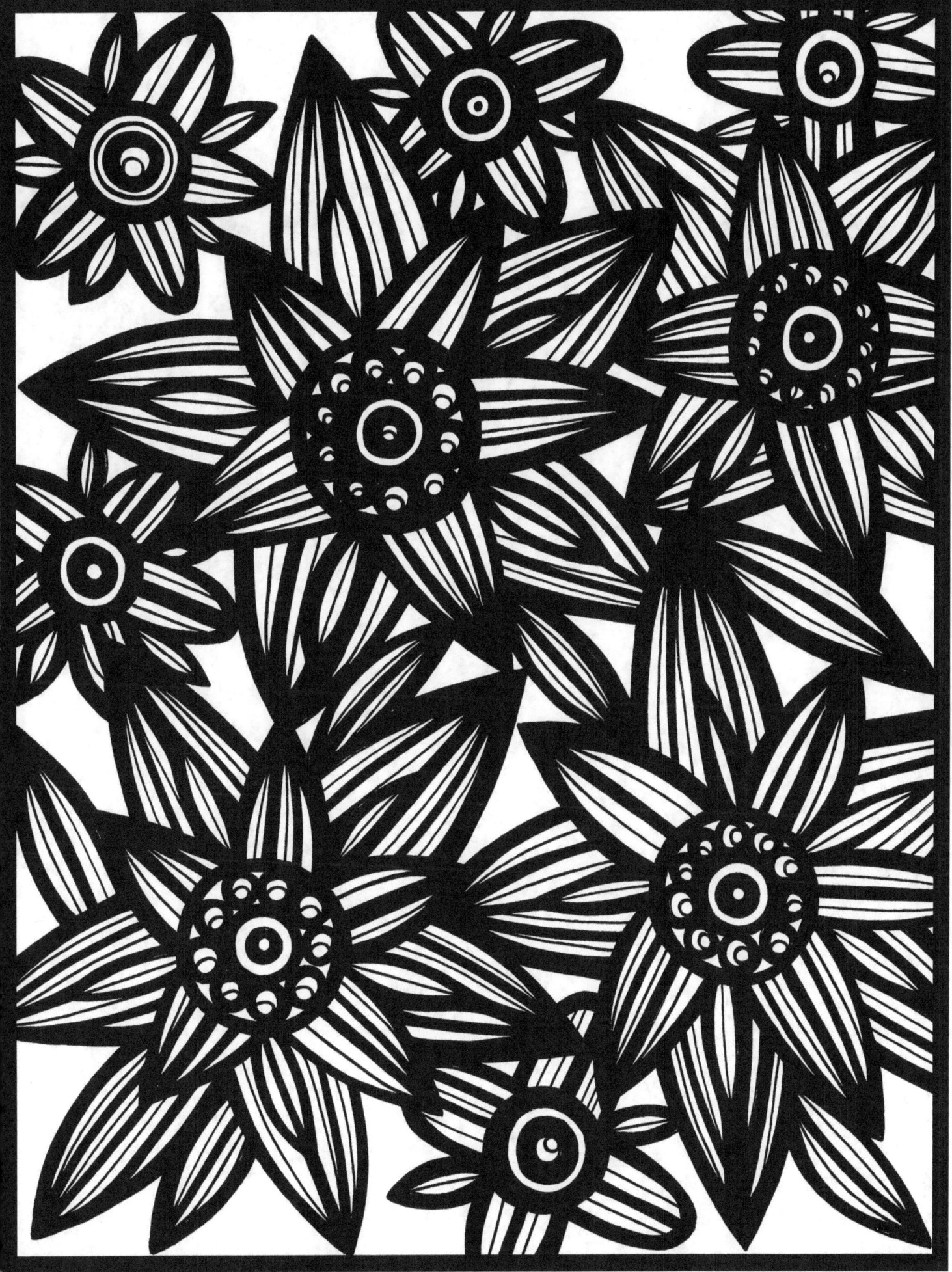

THE END, THANK YOU.

COPYRIGHT 2020
BY EDDIE ALFARO
ALL RIGHTS RESERVED.

MORE BOOKS:
631ART.COM

www.ingramcontent.com/pod-product-compliance
Lightning Source LLC
Chambersburg PA
CBHW080131240526
45468CB00009BA/2368